Charred

Published October 2020 by Team Angelica Publishing,
an imprint of Angelica Entertainments Ltd

Team Angelica Publishing
51 Coningham Road
London W12 8BS

www.teamangelica.com

A CIP catalogue record for this book is available from
the British Library

ISBN 978-1-9163561-2-2

Charred

a survivor speaks her truth to inspire

Andreena Leeanne

TEAM
ANGE
LICA

Dedication

The most radical thing you can do is speak your truth and be your authentic self because there will only ever be one YOU.

This book is dedicated to YOU the reader, to my beautiful daughter Renée Walton, and to my hugely encouraging fiancé Germaine Joseph, who introduced me to poetry in 2014.

Foreword

There is strong correlation between childhood trauma and mental health issues. I suffer with PTSD and depression, and use poetry to write honestly about the multitude of issues I have experienced in my 39 years. I have found writing to be hugely therapeutic. While I recognize the value of professional therapy, my poetry has helped me to come to terms with some of these issues.

If they're not already doing so, I hope to inspire the readers of this book to speak and write their truth. We don't have to be qualified writers to write down how we feel – honesty is the only qualification for this kind of work – and we don't have to share it unless we want to.

This collection is called *Charred*. Think of a piece of wood that has been exposed to the flames. You may think of it as damaged – and it's true it has been burnt and blackened – but it is still resilient, and much stronger after going through this process.

Think of me as a piece of charred wood.

Andreena Leeanne.

Table of Contents

Speak your truth

It's okay to laugh
it's okay to cry
it's okay to hide
it's okay, take time
it's gonna hurt
speak your truth

it's okay to feel
it's okay to bleed
it's okay to weep
it's okay, go deep
it's gonna hurt
speak your truth

it's okay to hug
it's okay to love
it's okay to fight
it's okay to resist
it's gonna hurt
speak your truth

it's okay to be open
it's okay to be broken
it's okay to be vulnerable

Andreena Leeanne

people may not like it
people may not like you
people may not like themselves
it's gonna hurt
speak your truth.

Umpteen years and counting

These umpteen years have not been bliss

most days it has been hit and miss to be honest

life taking the proverbial piss

things and time changes, various ranges, people and places

life comes and goes in different stages

umpteen chapters in the same book

I am so open take a look

not just at the cover

the pages inside

the writing

the binding front and back

until I decide to give myself the sack

believe me I have contemplated it several times

cries for help

failed attempts

more cries for help

Andreena Leeanne

yet I am still here trying to survive

maintaining the people and things that keep me alive

at times, I want to die

breathe my very last breath

flatten out my chest so I can take a very long rest

what looks rosy on the outside has deep-rooted scars on the
    inside

and let's face it, we will carry those scars for the rest of our
    lives.

My mind

The mind is a powerful tool

it should be on the national curriculum

we don't learn enough about it at school

life experiences and stress often get my head in a mess

I find ways to de-stress, unwind and clear my mind

with mindfulness, meditation, relaxation and long walks in
the park

staring at the trees and the green grass

until at last

my mind is clear for a bit Then life sets in and it takes
another hit

it's like my mind knows what triggers to press in the end

work, family, friends and transport issues drive me round
the bend

for me living in London town

my life is full of ups and downs

sometimes things are nice, and things go right

other times it's shit and that's just the reality of it

I love life and living is what I love the most about life

I know I've got to take care of myself

put myself first in real terms

my health is my wealth as a wise person once told me

being mentally healthy is one of my top priorities

I'll try my best to set aside my fears and park any negativity
from self and others

and be the best me that I can be.

Charred

Anxiety and stress

Over the past few months I have been experiencing high
      intensity anxiety and stress

been feeling like important aspects of my life are in a mess

what the fucking heck?

I mean seriously

I've been getting this unrelenting pummelling pain in my
      neck

the more I try to concentrate and think positive thoughts

the more it feels like my neck pain, anxiety and stress are
      working in cahoots

if you know me well and you are reading this

you're probably thinking I'm taking the piss

from the outside looking in my life looks bliss

you're probably counting my numerous possessions

examining my beautiful family unit

somewhat successful career

Poetry LGBT, my creative open mic baby

Andreena Leeanne

I beg you

look past all of that and focus on these facts

I'm telling you now

I found it hard to cope

although not at the stage where I would contemplate a rope

I tried mindfulness, meditation, relaxation, long walks in the
park

but my mind worked overtime

I found it extremely hard to keep my thoughts in line

for now, I will say no more about that gigantic sore head

they say time is a healer and

with time

it passed and I was able to see the other side of the grass.

Charred

Were you there?

Life is either positive or negative

depending on how you look at it

it's black, white or grey

until you put some colour in

depending on your eyesight

it's dim or bright

blurred vision day and night

you can either see in the dark or see in the light

what happens in the dark always comes to light

seeing is believing

20/20 vision

hindsight

right

did you hear my insides cry when I was five?

the tears in my tear ducts have dried up from

all the tears I cried night after night

Andreena Leeanne

did you see my heart bleed when she left me to be with him?

were you there to touch that blood blistered spot?

when that scalding cup of water spilled on my lap?

were you there when I took 12 pills one by one?

cried for help

left for dead

and lived

were you there when this happened and that happened?

were you there when that happened, and this happened?

I could go on and on, but I won't

though the past is the past

it often comes back to haunt, taunt and flaunt itself

like it belongs in the present

I like presents

fill me with gifts

let my cup overflow with the giving

did you see how like magic with time

Charred

my eyes light up when I smile

ask me how I'm doing today

I'm fine

I'm alive.

Abortion

You would have been 22

I never stop thinking of you

you live on in my mind

my unborn child

I too was a child

you deserve more words than this

you deserved to live.

Charred

I try so hard at life

I do everything I can all of the time to occupy my mind

in order to forget

over the years Mum has told me to forgive and forget

my mind won't allow me to forget

and my body so fragile at that time won't allow me to forgive

I have tried to put it all behind me and live

I don't think I will ever forgive

my life now is not that hard

but my past life is scarred

charred

blackened like tar

if only I could go for a lifelong drive in my car

I try so hard at life every time so I can forgive and forget

Mum said 'what's done is done, now move on'

I have moved on

Andreena Leeanne

at least until something goes wrong

and brings me back

or something goes right

I feel like I don't deserve that delight

this plight has no end in sight

and I don't think I will ever be alright.

Charred

Child abuse

All children are precious

their little hearts, body and minds are precious

to the ones whose innocence was taken away from a early

   age

I hear you

it happened to me too

I believe you

what happens in the dark in the night or at any time

will eventually come to light

it takes time

young child

what can we do

right now to help you?

you probably don't have all the words to articulate what's

   happening to you

it's child abuse

it's disgusting

it sickens my stomach to know you are hurting

at 5 my fragile body was scarred

I empathise, and know that what you are going through right

   now is hard

those people who hurt us make life more challenging for us

Andreena Leeanne

I can't make any promises to you but I can say
life doesn't have to be this hard
though it will be hard to find people to trust
this situation is extremely tough
the pandemic is taking its toll on all of us in different ways

I wish I could save you

we all need to look deep inside
to see what's happening behind closed doors
for me it happened at home
the place that's meant to be safe and secure was the place my
              virginity was taken away
young child
I want to help you
so many barriers prevent us from helping you
someone needs to save you
it doesn't matter what anyone in your future says
you are brave
courage comes in many forms
you are courageous
something needs to be done to help you NOW!
but how?

Charred

My poetry is my therapy

Every time I feel sad, I reach for my note pad

I write a few lines and instantly it clears my mind

sometimes I'm filled with so much emotion

to me, writing is some kind of potion

when I put pen to paper everything seems much clearer

ink bleeding

I no longer need to pay for counselling

or indeed take any medicine

through my sad times

I write poetry that (sometimes) rhymes

the pen connecting with the paper

I feel so much safer

with every letter of the alphabet

sometimes when I'm finished, I'm dripping with sweat

heart racing, finger on pen pacing

vocabulary flowing

like a river gushing

Andreena Leeanne

no need for rushing

take time

everything will be just fine

my life encourages me to write poetry

because to me...

it's my saving grace, my counselling, my therapy.

Charred

I write

I appear larger than life, but life is much larger than me

it's hard to see, behind the bubbles and smiles,

the heavy burdens on my mind at times

I smile to keep the struggles at bay

and remain busy to stay alive

most of the time

at times I cry inside

a word

an image

a memory

something little or nothing can trigger it

writing saves me temporarily

the pen cradles my emotions

as the ink bleeds onto the paper

the process lightens the burden

it helped in the past to try counselling

Andreena Leeanne

to open up and talk

someday I will again

for now, I choose to sit in silence and write it down.

Charred

Self doubting

One day I would like my poetry to heal the nation

but for now, it's just creative procrastination

to me, my poems aren't ever good enough

I'm just going by what I'm hearing

it's so hard to stop comparing

some say don't worry Andreena

you'll get better with age

practice makes perfect

and perfection may bring me satisfaction

I put aside my nerves and stage fright

and keep going to these poetry nights

to seek out attention and to get a reaction

more concentration on my craft

may stop me feeling so daft

reaching deep into my soul

I will one day reach my goal

Andreena Leeanne

to heal the nation

with the stories I hold waiting to be told

my truth is pure unrelenting gold

that needs to be shared before I get old.

Charred

Happiness

I urge you to find happiness in the little things

because happiness is short-lived

put aside your troubles and strife

we only have one life

life is too short for regrets

grab the people next to you and

send texts

have sex

make mess

take time to say hi how's life?

it costs nothing to be polite

make time to give

find happiness in the little things

because happiness is short lived.

2 weeks in Jamaica

My grandad was ill
I went to see him in Jamaica
St Ann is a small parish and Green Hill is where he lived
everyone knows everyone
and everyone knew him
I was outed before I got there
by my ex husband and his new wife
to him, me being a lesbian carried more shame than his wife
        being white
this place was proper ignorant
I almost died from his gossip lips
he threw me under the bus and waged a war between us
I had heard a story about a man called John
who was whipped and beaten after being caught with
        another man
this happened before my time
but homophobia is rife now in Jamaica as it was in that time
I feared for my life
I almost didn't board the 8-hour flight
whilst on the plane I passed the time
listening to Emeli Sandé on rewind
the same songs playing over and over again
thoughts going round and round in my head

Charred

Jamaica is well known for its obeah and its homophobia
the country has more churches per square mile than any-
      where else in the world
I cried
I'm a sinner
and living in sin is how I felt within
Heaven's doors will never open to let me in
the plane landed
I took a taxi and drove for miles through the night
Jamaica, what a heavenly sight
moonshine so bright
morning came and there was so much to explain
I was questioned by grandad's helper, she asked:
why?
you weren't brought up this way
it's dem mad people ah England leading you astray
the shame
meanwhile on the news
two men were found hanged and bound
homophobia was all around.
she continued
the questions flooded in, along with insults thrown like
      rockstone:
why you style your hair like man?
God made Adam and Eve not Adam and Steve
I wanted to leave but I had nowhere to go

Andreena Leeanne

if I stepped outside, I knew I'd be questioned more
I stayed inside for 2 weeks until it was time to leave
I didn't see Jamaica in all its glory
the sea breeze
the palm trees
I stayed inside bombarded with questions
a battleground
at least Grandad was too ill to care
he was just happy to see me there
I returned home feeling weak as I had failed to speak
speak up for what's right.

Charred

Conversion therapy

You tried and tried to change my life

because that's what you think is right

some of us don't put up a fight because you have convinced

     us

what you think is right

some of us are living a lie until they die

because you have made them terrified

is there really a heaven and hell in sight?

I refuse to let you ruin my life

I love my soon-to-be wife

we don't need your conversion therapy

leave us be

we don't interfere with what you wear and how you style

     your hair

so get the fuck outta here

we don't tell you who to love

who to fuck

who to trust

and who to be around

so get the fuck out of town

we don't want you around

to make us feel bound to your hetero normative 'normality'

your theories and ideologies are outdated and utterly wrong

wake up

I've got news for you

the world is moving on.

Charred

Inner voice

There was a voice inside waiting to be heard

hidden thoughts and feelings far from absurd

holding back the tears for so many years

due to negative judgement and fears

fear of being rejected

fear of being isolated

fear of being violated

fear of people with their unrelenting hatred

fear of feeling that if I stayed confined

I would eventually lose my mind

buried deep inside

there was nowhere left to hide

that inner voice needed to come out

it needed to bellow and shout:

I too am worthy in all my human glory.

Andreena Leeanne

Now & then

Back in the day when I was single

free as a bird and ready to mingle

all the butch girls would make me tingle

oh my

those were the days

since then I have changed my ways

the one has come along

in her arms is where I belong

she captured my heart right from the start

I pray nothing and no one tears us apart

lesbo land can be very fickle

just ask Lady Pumpernickel

she thought her relationship would last

if you see her now, it's all in the past.

Charred

Masculine woman

I am woman

she too is woman

I love my woman

she looks like a man

wears men's clothes

has a deep voice

often gets a rough time outside

'Excuse me! Didn't you see this is the ladies' loo?'

yes I did

she replied

I too am woman

small as they are

look at my tits

now put that in your pipe and smoke it.

Just us

When I breathe the air I breathe, you breathe it with me
and I beg you not to leave
it's just us
when after the rain comes a thunderstorm
it's not you it's me that keeps us safe and warm
don't sound the alarm and pull the plug
hold me close and give me a hug
it's just us
trust
this relationship could easily crumble into dust
because we are existing without lust
it's been you and me for months
just us
I need you to believe in me

and wait for me to deal with the things that are plaguing me
I need you to see this is real but not our reality
not based on vanity but based purely on love and loyalty
just give me some time

to bring back the sunshine in my smile
I promise you

it will be worth your while.

Charred

Fucking Facebook

I used to be one of those girlfriends who was affectionate
      first thing in the morning and last thing at night
these days it's my fucking phone getting all the glory and
      delight
constantly checking my Facebook morning, noon and night
      I've got an addictive personality
although that's no excuse
I could use this to my advantage in the bedroom and put it to
      good use
I'll leave this space blank for you to use your imagination
to muster up some wonderful creation
relationships need affection and stability
all that good stuff as well as agility
I'm aware of my changed ways
I'm looking forward to better days
let's see what tonight brings
fuck you fucking Facebook
you antisocial thing
I shall ignore you if you buzz, beep, squeak or ring

tonight, it will be you and me, my love.

Andreena Leeanne

Touch me, touch you not

I want to squeeze you, tease you

lick you from your head to your toes

but I can't do that
you're a touch me not

touch me
touch you not
my hands are kept behind my back

I want to kiss you on your neck and caress your back
I want to fuck you with a dildo and
strap you with a strap
but I can't do that
you're a touch me not

touch me
touch you not
my hands are kept behind my back

I want to soak you in bath salts
rub you down with oil and suck on those breasts
but I can't do that
you're a touch me not

Charred

I let you fuck me, suck me, finger me and do what you want
but when it comes to me doing it back, you're like
oh no you can't do that
you're a touch me not

touch me
touch you not
I love you lots and lots
with my hands kept behind my back.

Andreena Leeanne

Sex and love

The other day we spoke about sex and I got angry and said
I don't even wana talk about sex because if I start I'm gonna
get vex

we communicate now and again by text
how is that the language of love?
when I ask you for a cuddle
your head is in a muddle
my head is already at foreplay
touch me, tease me and lead me astray

she said I'm sorry
okay
I didn't know you felt this way
that very moment the convo

turned from no sex vex to steamy rough sex
shut the bedroom door
our clothes torn off and in a mess on the floor
kissing, biting, touching, caressing grabbing, sucking, licking
before we knew it the toys came out and we were
screaming, heavy breathing, moaning and groaning
sounded like we had started a war in that bedroom
I didn't want to cum any time before noon

Charred

that very day I wanted us to stay in that bedroom forever and
bond
bond like glue
consummate our relationship until we both knew
that we are like finger and glove
we are very much in love.

Andreena Leeanne

It's not what it is... it's what we make it

We love to love and love to hate

who we get with, is it fate?

what we think about is what we attract

think too much and we start to subtract

we don't need people who make us feel feeble

we need to change that feeble to achievable

we must admit when we are wrong

when we become one, we stand up strong

in my humble opinion

a relationship is not that complicated

it's simply what we make it.

Charred

I was your meat and now you're vegan

I was your meat but now you're vegan

you cast me aside

swept me out on the tide

in your eyes I'll be gone till November

in my eyes and my heart, I will return

the day after never

why?

because I am never coming back

not even to fill the gap, the crack

you will have some of those

ask this person and that person

and so and so

I don't need to mention their names because they know

and you know who they are because they have been on the
   receiving end

of your psychological blows

Andreena Leeanne

what you continue to do is wrong

I feel down now but not for long

I will recover from this

it's like the chorus of a really sad song

that goes around and around in my head,

like a relationship that is dead

I was your meat and now you're vegan

on repeat

I was your meat.

Charred

Bare faced fakery

How dare you speak to me so sweetly

only to frown when you turn your back to me

that's what I call bare faced fakery

the other day I told you good news

the look on your face

you seemed bemused

you caught my gaze and smiled back at me

that's what I call bare faced fakery

I wish you would be honest

instead of being fake

I really don't know how much more of this I can take

it's no surprise

to hear from someone else that you pray for my demise

please!

no more two-faced lies, I cried.

Friend or foe

I wear my heart on my sleeve

you want to bring me to my knees

I lay all my cards on the table

you want to hang me with a cable

wrap it tight around my neck

and while I'm gasping for air

you add insult to injury

and pull on my hair

as if the pain wasn't enough

you strut your stuff acting rough and tough

you're supposed to be my friend

ride or die until the end you said

I keep your secrets in a locket I wear close to my heart

I never dreamt of tearing our friendship apart

but this cannot continue

I am worth more than this

Charred

the people I meet these days are just hit and miss

friend or foe?

not your average Joe

the seeds you plant

you will reap what you sow

karma is a bitch

for what goes around usually comes around

and you will find yourself buried deep underground

with no one to love you

no one to hug you

all alone

set in stone

someone else will come along to sit on your throne.

Andreena Leeanne

Workmate//No mate

I heard so much about you

I was so glad to finally meet you

you seemed so nice when I came to greet you

6 months on

that façade was gone

time passed and I got to know you at last

workmate? No mate

you're just a sneaky little rattlesnake

you shit stir and you bitch

you are nothing but a snitch

the feeling was mutual but at work it was business as usual

months later we gladly parted ways

I no longer had to be intimidated by your gaze

more time passed

my freedom didn't last like a blast from the past

we meet again.

Charred

you boast about how you won the tender

all I can think about is going on a bender

bring on Fridays

wishing my life away

my commitments force me to stay in the job I adore

with a manager I hate

I'm committed to my wifey and daughter

can't feed them on bread and water

workmate? No mate

this can't be fate for you to fill my days so full of hate

you are the only one who makes me feel like this

before I met you

my life was bliss.

Andreena Leeanne

Facebook letter to my sister

Long lost sister found then lost again in no time

not my choice but hers

not my loss but hers

scrap that

we are both losers in the family game

this situation is insane

the other siblings I am yet to meet

I've told myself to forget it

my heartstrings are not meant for this

kiss little man for me

my 2 nieces and 1 nephew who I never got the chance to

know

you will reap what you sow

maybe things have worked out for the best

it's not me who is being put to the test

though I'm glad I got to know you at last

you true colours didn't take long to show

jealousy was it?

Charred

that slimy green glow

I'm done with this

not going over it anymore

the future is here

you will soon be in the past

history

a solved mystery

I wish you all the best sis

honestly.

Andreena Leeanne

No seasons, no reasons, no lifetime

We were not related by blood, but we were family

I was always there when you needed me

we were once like Siamese twins

although never joined at the hip

look at us now

like two passing ships

I thought about begging you to stay

come what may

now I am begging you to walk away

this ain't working for me

This ain't working for us

no seasons, no reasons, no lifetime

this friendship has reached the end of the line

it has run its course

I'm done flogging this dead horse

I meant to say this to you face to face

Charred

since I no longer take pride of place

I hardly see your face

I did try to call you

you didn't pick up the phone

that was no surprise really

as I'm no longer your favourite ring tone

no disrespect

it's not my style

I'm down with the times

which is why I sent you this by text.

Andreena Leeanne

You changed like the weather

I've known you for ages

I thought we were close

we rolled together in all types of weather

I never thought you would do me wrong

I always thought we would stay strong

on the day that you betrayed me

if I were a Christian

I would have prayed

I never saw it coming

I always thought you were stunning

well I never

you changed like the weather

since you've been gone better days have come along

hell suits you

you're at home where you belong.

Charred

High without a kite

I'm alright

I'm fine

things get better with time

until then I will toe this line

have no fear my dears

spring is here

birds and butterflies fly in the air

air in my lungs

deep breaths in and deep breaths out

getting ready for when I'm out and about

you'll soon see and hear me shout

you'll soon see and hear me roar

soar

high without a kite

I'll regain my wings and tings

set free my sins

and win.

Andreena Leeanne

Body Mass Index

Who do you think you are? Poking fun at my weight

when your face is in such a sorry state

wait

I'm not stooping as low as you – I

may have a high BMI

but my loving ways have no limits like the sky

who do you think you are? Coming at me with your
corruption

with your poisonous words of body mass destruction

instead of being a supportive mate

you continue to demotivate

really

who do you think you are?

can you not see your words are causing me pain?

all I want to do is eat again and again

I wear my scars on the inside

Charred

deep down inside is where I try to hide

you know what

forget you

I am going to be me and try to forgive the people who judge

because in my skin is where I live.

Smile through the pain

These braces are putting me through my paces

it hurts to smile and hurts to frown

these braces are turning my life upside down

I wasn't blessed to get them done on the NHS

they said I was too old and it's just cosmetic

I said to the dentist stop being pathetic

and stormed out of the clinic

on the way out I saw a poster for Six Month Smiles and
smiled

it looked really neat, so I had it done at the dentist right up
my street

in this land of milk and honey

I have spent so much money

trying not to look like Bugs Bunny

even though I went private

it feels very much public

out and about people stare into my mouth

Charred

it even hurts to shout

some say they know how I'm feeling

really?

you don't know the half of it

I can't eat what I like

they're wound so tight

I go to bed crying every night

this painful sacrifice is preventing me from eating my
favourite

mackerel and rice

instead it's baby food and soup

I may need counselling to recoup

I cannot wait to be released from this ball and chain

never to return to this pain again

in six months' time, this will all be in the past

and I will have the perfect smile at last.

Andreena Leeanne

Home

18 years old

no home, no abode

no place for me to go

standing outside in the cold on what felt like the front line

the Earth stood still

as I cried and cried

nowhere left for me to run and nowhere to hide

I slept in the park

slept in an abandoned car

it was dark

a really dark time

no home, no abode

no place for me to go

I moved across London

found new friends

Charred

sofa today, sofa tomorrow but

I was out of the ends

fertile womb

empty room

loneliest time of my life

pure doom and gloom

although this time was different

a room in a shared house

I even shared the room with a mouse

it ran over my foot one day as I stood up

I screamed for days

the year was 2002

womb filled up

bun in the oven

given a temporary place

bed and breakfast was provided

Andreena Leeanne

my head and heart were divided

roof over my head but still no friends

as this place too was not in my ends

luckily, I had learned to fend for myself

time flew

baby bump grew

started eating for two

and before I knew it

I was offered a flat

small

one bed

first floor with my very own front door

finally

a place to call my own

comfort, sanity, privacy

filled it with stuff

Charred

ran up some debts

it was a mess

yes

it was messy at times

especially when my head wasn't in my right mind

the year was 2010

notice of seeking possession

out on my ear again

temporary accommodation

Tottenham

again, not in my ends

they say history does repeat itself again and again

Mum was homeless when she was young too

for the most part, we stuck to her like glue

temporary home, almost abode

somewhere to call home

Andreena Leeanne

for 6 months at least

sleeping on the same bedsheets for weeks

then I got the call

it's a 2 bed with a garden

and best of all it's permanent

somewhere safe to rest our heads

ground floor

once again

my very own front door

there's no place like home.

Charred

My first Christmas at 33

32 Christmases already came and went

but this one was special

my first Christmas at 33

the first time it wasn't all about me

feeling motionless, sad and lonely

my first real Christmas at 33

with tonnes of presents under the tree

most belonging to me, my daughter and my wife to be

for the first time ever, I am filled with glee

to be with my newly made family

I feel like I belong

gone are the days of playing that old sad song

this year has been a roller coaster journey

with many twists and turns

pain from supposed to be loved ones

emotional sores as painful as acid burns

Andreena Leeanne

Christmas is an emotional time of year

this one is the first to end with a cheer

feeling hopeful to see what the next one has in store

filled with love and hope I spend it with the ones I adore

bring on December

with my new digital camera

I'll capture new memories

forever and ever.

Charred

Morphemstow

Walthamstow is morphing into Hackney

Amsterdam cycle lanes for days

these roads were not designed that way

parking restrictions

closed roads

20 mile per hour zones

dead end turns as anger burns

'it's better for our future' I hear you cry

'our carbon footprints are massive when we fly'

dozens of posh shops and coffee shops

why?

big names like Tesco and Co-op suffocate our corner shops

it's all corporate capitalism gone mad

what's happening to our social spaces?

our parks?

what's happening to social housing?

'for the many not the few' they said

fuck you is what I hear them whisper in my ear

what about us?

there's no one we can trust

for these are lies

in front of our very own eyes

Andreena Leeanne

while these major cities form, and posh shops become the
        norm
we will be separated from our spawn
the youngsters of today
I feel it for their future but for now
while Walthamstow is morphing into Hackney
for better or for worse
life as we know it goes on
until we 'the many' rise up with a plan.

Charred

Home for me is/Homeowner

Call me a gentrifier
if house prices increase blame me
but it took courage and guts to get a foot on this rung
though it's another property gone
from the social housing stock
I've worked extremely hard to secure this rock
I did it to give my daughter a chance
to give her a better start
a foundation
somewhere secure that she can call her own
home for me is more than bricks and mortar
It's a warm place, an abundance of food, hot running water
a place I can be messy and make mess in 5 minutes
funny how much longer it takes to tidy up
and there's always washing up
home is a place I can be me
and unleash my creativity
home for me is a place to keep clean
a place to be proud, quiet and loud
a place to think and make plans
a place to bake bread alone
and choose to break it with family and friends
home for me is comfort, safety and sanity

Andreena Leeanne

everything in its entirety
somewhere safe to return to
a place where I can hide behind closed doors
or keep them open if I like
home for me is choice
freedom to shop and choose things I like
things you may not think are nice
home for me is a place to rest my head at any time
and unwind with candlelight at night
home for me is the only place and space
where I can do what I like and it's alright
after all that I have been through
I am lucky to be alive
and live in the place I have just described
proud homeowner
call me a gentrifier
If house prices increase
blame me.

Charred

Covid-19 in silence

Stay at home in silence

protect the NHS and save lives in silence

shop for basic necessities in silence

exercise once per day in silence

travel for work where you cannot work from home in silence

if you have symptoms

a high temperature

contagiously cough in silence

stay at home for 7 days in silence

stay at home for 14 days in silence

once the days have passed and the symptoms have ended,

still stay silent

70 and over

silence

underlying health conditions

silence

pregnant

silence

support for businesses and workers

silence

action taken to protect lives and incomes in silence

loans and guarantees in silence

tax relief in silence

cash grants in silence

employees can receive 80% of their income in silence then

employees can receive 60% in silence

mortgage holidays of 3 months in silence

read the UK government guidance leaflet where this

        information came from in silence

further information is available online

in silence.

Charred

Black Lives Matter (stop killing us)

We who are Black have been under attack for centuries
check your history
slavery
the colour of our skin and the texture of our hair have made
        us enemies
the bombs thrown
wars in countries around the world
the guns
put them down
the knives
young lives are disappearing before our eyes
the countless arrests
a knee pressed down on his neck
George Floyd was his name
another brother gone too soon
dead
let us live
let us live
black lives matter
all lives matter yes
but it is black lives being lost en masse
tell me
what have we done to deserve this fate?

Andreena Leeanne

it can't be right that the melanin in our skin is the cause of so
            much hate
this racism has to stop
generations lost
please
stop killing us
we can't catch a break
we can't catch our breath
we can't breathe
let us breathe
don't stay silent
help us fight this
we matter
yes
we matter
BLACK LIVES MATTER.

Same difference

Stare at me please, I like it

check out my hair

it's the texture of rough cotton before it's relaxed

stare at me please

my brows are a few shades darker than yours

my lashes shade and protect my eyes as yours do yours

look into my eyes

tear ducts in their corners

where tears fall, stream and gush

stare at me please, I like it

check out my nose as it's uncommonly smaller than yours

check out my lips: – they too were made to kiss and pout the
occasional lipstick

tell me if we don't breathe the same way

as I take a gulp of air into my lungs and breathe out

my neck, my arms, my elbows

this finger too awaits that special ring

my breasts

my back

cut me some slack as you check out my fat

now focus on my feet

they're more or less the same as yours

10 toes, arched, heels and a callus or two

Andreena Leeanne

me, you, they, her and him

please

check out my skin

sweet shea buttered melanin

cut me deep and see if we don't breathe the same way

see if my blood goes from dark to red when it hits the bed

stare at me please, I like it

white, black, yellow, purple or blue

I stare at you too

yes

so many similarities

now you tell me if we're so different.

Charred

Badmind people gweh

Me love life and living is what mi love the most about life
as we try to live in peace and harmony
the devil send people to badder we
dem a watch and dem a pree
and a tink to dem self
why good tings always happen to she and not me?
dem must not know bout doing good fi good tings to follow
either dat or dem heart hollow
dutty grudgeful badmind people will never succeed
cah dem try fi bring good people to dem knees
what dem need fi do ah wash out dem mind wid conditioner
        and Febreeze
ask di doctor to operate pon dem heart fi mek it clean
and stop being mean
di year soon finish and a next one soon start
mek sure you a walk wid good tings inna you heart
as di saying goes
'today a fi you and tomorrow a fi mi'
so gwarn do you ting and no badder wid me.

Andreena Leeanne

People and life eh

People eh

life eh

they say I'm a sight for sore eyes

right now, my heart is sore

I fear I'll feel like this forever more

let's settle the score

you hated me

I cared for you

not today

no more

I have shed the last tear

this is so last year

now it's time to get myself in gear

don't come near

leave me be

to grieve this loss

Charred

in peace

who gives a toss?

I do

well at least I used to

I must get over you

this situation

I sleep

I wake

the sun goes up and down

day after day

week after week

moving on feels long

wait

the penny dropped

pick it up

take a seat

replenish

Andreena Leeanne

eat

breathe

replenish

live

repeat

succeed

people eh

life eh.

Charred

In my humble opinion

These are not based on factual information

it's not a condemnation

these are merely my opinions

in my opinion some people are lucky

is there such a thing as luck?

or is it just preparation meets opportunity?

in my opinion life is a gift

eggs and sperm meet in the womb to create it

or you, me, her and him would not be brought into this life of
        sin

in my opinion

there should be no religion

we should believe in what we want to believe in

what our minds can conceive, we can achieve

in my opinion some people use social networks to network

others use them to chat and to flirt

some people log on to fit into society's version of normality

this is not reality

whilst some create a new identity

in my opinion people need hugs

they need to be told daily they are loved

especially my daughter who has one father and two mums

as I said in the beginning, these are merely my opinions

you can tell me yours

doesn't mean I will listen

you may even see my eyes glaze over

this brings me on to selfish people...

in my opinion these people care about themselves and no
one else

they are only interested in what you can do for them

well, all I can say is they can go to hell

on the other hand – in my opinion

this world is full of lovely people

people who attend poetry nights to get an insight into other
people's lives

Charred

in my opinion some of us are filled with so much pain and
        emotion

we're scared to let it out, so we write with pure devotion

this final one however is not my opinion

this is a fact

I am one of those people trying to keep my life intact.

Andreena Leeanne

No longer keeping secrets

I was sexually abused from the age of five

yes, the innocent and tender age of five

not long was I alive on this Earth

when my mum met that six-foot sex offender in Jamaica

that's when I learned to keep secrets

I was his little secret

at 7 I begged her not to marry him, but she did and years
later

had the cheek to blame me for ruining her marriage

when we returned to England, she sent for him soon after

she said I should have told her

I said, How could I? I was just a child

Leroy Channer is his name and today at 38 I am no longer
ashamed.

to this day that woman still carries his last name

knowing what that man did to me for 5 years

Charred

at 9 he tried to pass me to his friend whose name I think
begins with M

looking back, it makes me cringe to think I was almost part
of a paedophile ring

she could never say she didn't know because it was her who
caught him in the act

she could not lie or deny because she saw me on top of him
with her very own eyes

it was her who called the police

he was arrested, convicted and spent a short time inside

she accepted a wooden prison gift handcrafted by him

she saw him when he was released

she had him in her car within 3 miles of our street

the betrayal

the deceit

his punishment far from fit the crime as it's me who is doing
the time

throughout the years I have tried to forgive and forget

this I will never forget

live and let live yes and maybe with time forgive

Andreena Leeanne

years ago, Mum told me to forgive him and move on and
that's when I decided to keep quiet

I decided not to speak even when others confided in me what
had happened to them

how can I ever forgive a man who almost ruined my life
several times?

I'm not just talking about the times I tried to end my life

I'm talking about the times I could not be touched by the
people I claimed to love

I'm talking about the times I slept around so much I was
labelled a slut

I'm talking about the times I drank so much I got
ridiculously drunk

I'm talking about never fully knowing who to trust

the antidepressants

the time I've lost thinking about this I will never get back

I'm talking about watching my own daughter like a hawk and
teaching her from birth to tell me if someone ever
touched her here, here or here (pointing to private
parts)

at times I relive the physical, psychological and emotional
pain and I'm aware it will never fully go away

some of my relationships have really suffered over the years

Charred

I will always be scarred, charred

it has been traumatic to say the least

to say I've been through a lot in my life is an understatement

I have been through heaps

the PTSD

hours of lost sleep

wide awake night after night counting sheep

over time I have been able to see the wood for the trees

statistics show that 1 in 4 women and 1 in 6 men are affected
 by this

I am a woman

I am resilient

I am courageous

I have achieved amazing things

despite my circumstances I remain strong

I now know full well what he did was wrong

I am not to blame

after telling Mum I'm now speaking out

Andreena Leeanne

her response is still to keep quiet and move on

he has 5 children she said

what are you after, revenge?

I know she's only trying to safeguard herself

don't silence me – I will no longer be silent

the silence is broken, the worms have been released from the
can

you failed to protect me Mum and now you've washed your
hands

I am nobody's little secret; I no longer keep these kinds of
secrets

I will speak my truth

it's my truth to speak no matter how much havoc it wreaks

I'm done protecting you, I need to look out for me

I can't turn back time, but I can spend my time fighting for
what's right

to ensure others can speak of their plight as I continue to
write.

Solidarity

Me one, me too, me three

we are not free until we are all free

what happened to you

what happened to me

cannot go unseen

we are not free until we are all free

adding my voice to the conversation

I will not be silenced

don't silence me

I will speak

I will be heard

we are not free until we are all free

this is solidarity.

Andreena Leeanne

I am free

I spent my teenage years listening to lyrics like Buju Banton's
       'boom bye bye inna batty boy head'
what he's saying is gay people should be shot in the head
imagine that
those lyrics were heard by millions
in those days it never made me angry
in fact I used to dance to it
I could name a few more
TOK, Elephant Man, Vybz Kartel
in the 90s those tunes dominated the dance floor within my
       bedroom walls
in 1999 I married a man
was I in denial?
threesome anyone?
yes me, him and she
I came out as a lesbian in 2003
looking back all the clues were there; it was just me that
       couldn't see
people knew I was gay before me
It must have been the way I looked at my friend's auntie
or the way I dressed and rebelled by shaving my head
or maybe because I rode a moped
the truth is I chose not to see

Charred

I was too afraid to be true to me

people were too judgemental back then

I cared way too much about what people thought and said

I met a girl who took me to a gay club

those homophobic tunes were played by gay DJs in those gay
clubs

what a head fuck

people I knew said they liked the beat and ignored the lyrics

I'm not sure exactly when or why something changed

there was uproar

Buju and other bashment artists were banned

us gays had taken a stand

Out with that shit

it was no longer acceptable to listen to it

I no longer had to listen to it

they say I'm an activist

it's been a process

all part of the journey

I am free to finally be who I'm meant to be

loving living this reality within the LGBTQ+ community

my dysfunctional and disjointed family may not be proud of
me

but I'm able to maintain my sanity

and not let them get the better of me mentally

Andreena Leeanne

I'm gonna take a bow

    because I'm happy now.

Charred

Proud with Pride

Be proud and stand your ground

walk around and make your sound

wear your colours and stand out for hours

wave the various flags

try not to worry

find your tribe

you're in good company

shelter from the hate

fight with all your might for what is your human right

they will see

it's all love and light

in time we will all be alright

love who we love

marry who we marry

don't apologise

no need to ever be sorry

we are who we are

just live and be happy.

Changed

At the beginning of a particular year

I'm not ashamed to say

I didn't want to be around

but I feel differently now

spent too much time in my feelings

too much time in my head

I was an emotional mess

all the things that had happened to me had me

tumbling down

I couldn't hold a smile long before it turned into a

frown

I didn't want to be around

but I feel differently now

my family and friends didn't know how to help me at

the time

deep down I knew they wanted me around

they're the reason I'm still here feeling safe and

sound

not so long ago I didn't want to be around but look at

me now standing proud.

Charred

Sorry? Not sorry!

We all say sorry for this and sorry for that

there are some things I refuse to apologise for

sorry, not sorry I'm 5ft 2

sorry, not sorry I'm left-handed

sorry, not sorry I'm overweight

sorry, not sorry I'm black

sorry, not sorry I'm a lesbian

sorry, not sorry I'm a woman

not sorry for not being sorry

not sorry for my honesty

and definitely not sorry for being me

life is way too short

just be.

Speak your truth (reprise)

It's okay to laugh
it's okay to cry
it's okay to hide
it's okay, take time
it's gonna hurt
speak your truth

it's okay to feel
it's okay to bleed
it's okay to weep
it's okay, go deep
it's gonna hurt
speak your truth

it's okay to hug
it's okay to love
it's okay to fight
it's okay to resist
it's gonna hurt
speak your truth

it's okay to be open
it's okay to be broken

Charred

it's okay to be vulnerable

people may not like it

people may not like you

people may not like themselves

it's gonna hurt

speak your truth.

Andreena Leeanne

The time is now

When someone asks you the time
don't round it up or down
it's not nearly or almost anything
just say the time is NOW
I'm doing what's right for ME NOW
I'm working on making good food choices NOW
I'm checking in with how I feel NOW
I'm working on my happiness NOW
I'm nurturing my mind, body and soul NOW
I'm prioritising how I use my time NOW
I'm speaking my truth to inspire NOW
I'm seeking the professional help I need NOW
I'm connecting with my readers NOW
when you are asked for the time
don't round it up or down
it's time to take care of YOURSELF
when?
NOW.

Charred

Reflections...

Writing down how I feel has hugely changed my life.

I have included these lined pages for you to write whatever you like, in whatever style feels comfortable to you.

If you would like to share what you have written you can take a picture of it, send it to me and I will share it on my Instagram.

_____

_____

_____

_____

_____

_____

_____

_____

_____

_____

_____

_____

_____

_____

_____

Andreena Leeanne

Charred

Notes on self-care

Self-care may sometimes be seen as selfish and that's okay.
These are the things I do regularly for self-care. Feel free to
circle, tick, highlight or underline the ones you do, and also
feel free to add a few more.

Treat myself
Pamper myself
Practice gratitude
Meditate
Be present
Relax
Create quiet time
Play my handpan
Drink water
Sleep
Rest
Smile
Breathe deeply
Visit nature
Take time out
Walk
Set boundaries
Speak kindly to myself
Affirmations
Reflect on my achievements
Compliment myself
Love myself
Relaxing baths
Connect with friends
Connect with myself
Write
Digital detox
Social media detox
Declutter
Ask for help

Andreena Leeanne

About the author

 Andreena Leeanne, age 39, is an out and proud Black working-class Lesbian Poet, compère, inspirational speaker and mother to a teenage daughter. Born in Edgware, London, Andreena was sent to live with her grandparents in St Ann, Jamaica from age 1. At the age of 7 she returned to London and lived in several London boroughs with her mother. Andreena returned to Jamaica at age 17 to find herself, coming back to the UK at age 18 with a man she married at 19. Having been kicked out of home at 18, after experiencing a period of homelessness she eventually settled in the London Borough of Waltham Forest where, to cut a long story short, she currently lives with her fiancé, Germaine, and her 18-year-old daughter Renée. Andreena hopes to one day return to Jamaica, to challenge the extensive homophobia and culture of childhood sexual abuse that exists there.

Andreena writes and performs poetry to come to terms with and speak out about her personal experiences with homelessness, mental health, childhood sexual abuse and the many other challenges she has faced in her life. By speaking her truth, she hopes to inspire and empower others to speak their truth and take action.

In January 2015 Andreena founded Poetry LGBT Open Mic Night. Poetry LGBT is a warm and welcoming space for the LGBTQ+ community to come together to share their experiences through poetry and spoken word. It is a vital and much needed space for the LGBTQ+ community to share, create and express themselves. Andreena facilitates these sessions live at physical venues and online via Zoom.

Andreena delivers writing workshops online and in person, and often performs her poetry at community-led events, Labour Party events, and for local authorities such as the London Borough of Hackney during LGBT History Month, the Greater London Authority, and at International Women's Day events; and has had her work published in the anthology *Sista!* (Team Angelica, 2018).

In 2018 Andreena was one of Stonewall's Black History Month role models. Most recently she was delighted to be shortlisted by the National Diversity Awards as a Positive LGBT Role Model.

If you would like to get in touch, email:
Andreena1@hotmail.com

Hashtag: #charred

Instagram: @Survivor.Andreena.Leeanne

Follow @PoetryLGBT on Facebook, Twitter & Instagram

Email: poetryloungelgbt@hotmail.com

Useful contacts

Mind
Promotes the views and needs of people with mental health problems.
Phone: 0300 123 3393 (Monday to Friday, 9am to 6pm)
Website: www.mind.org.uk

Samaritans
Confidential support for people experiencing feelings of distress or despair.
Phone: 116 123 (free 24-hour helpline)
Website: www.samaritans.org.uk

NSPCC
Children's charity dedicated to ending child abuse and child cruelty.
Phone: 0800 1111 for Childline for children (24-hour helpline)
0808 800 5000 for adults concerned about a child (24-hour helpline)
Website: www.nspcc.org.uk

Victim Support
Phone: 0808 168 9111 (24-hour helpline)
Website: www.victimsupport.org

Family Lives
Advice on all aspects of parenting, including dealing with bullying.
Phone: 0808 800 2222 (Monday to Friday, 9am to 9pm and Saturday to Sunday, 10am to 3pm)
Website: www.familylives.org.uk

Relate
The UK's largest provider of relationship support.
Website: www.relate.org.uk

Charred

Shelter
Shelter believes everyone should have a home
Website: www.shelter.org.uk

The Outside Project
The UK's first LGBTIQ+ community shelter & centre
Website: www.lgbtiqoutside.org

Stonewall Housing
Safe spaces for LGBT+ people
Email: info@stonewallhousing.org
Phone: 020 7359 6242
Website: www.stonewallhousing.org

The Survivors Trust
National Umbrella Organisation for Specialist Rape and
Sexual Abuse Support Services
Website: www.thesurvivorstrust.org

Survivors UK
Support for male, trans & non-binary victims of sexual abuse
Phone: 020 3598 3898
Website: www.survivorsuk.org

One In Four UK
Supporting people who have experienced childhood sexual
abuse and trauma
Phone: 020 8697 2112
Website: www.oneinfour.org.uk

House of Rainbow
House of Rainbow (HOR) fosters relationships among Black,
Asian, Minority Ethnic (BAME), Lesbian, Gay, Bisexual,
Transgender, Intersex, Queer (LGBTIQ+) individuals, people
of faith and allies in order to create a safer and a more
inclusive community.
Website: www.houseofrainbow.org